To my good friend Sandy Fischer

Copyright © 1992 by Patricia Richardson Mattozzi
All rights reserved
First published in 1992 by Derrydale Books
distributed by Outlet Book Company, Inc.,
a Random House Company,
40 Engelhard Avenue
Avenel, New Jersey 07001

Manufactured in the United States

Designed by Melissa Ring

Library of Congress Cataloging-in-Publication Data
Mattozzi, Patricia.
My Father's world / by Patricia Richardson Mattozzi.
p.   cm.
ISBN 0-517-08144-X
1. Nature—Religious aspects—Christianity—Juvenile
literature.   I. Title.
BT695.5.M388   1992   92-12782
242'.62—dc20   CIP
AC

8   7   6   5   4   3   2   1

My Father's World

Patricia Richardson Mattozzi

Derrydale Books
New York • Avenel, New Jersey

My Father's world is beautiful
    He made it just for me,
And everywhere I look
    His wondrous touch I see.

The flowers nod their happy heads,
  A sweet smell fills the air,
Each petal painted carefully
  With tender loving care.

The brook that floats my sailing boat
And swirls between my toes,
Carries mountain water
Everywhere she flows.

And how wise our Father is
He seems to always know
When to send the gentle rain
And seal it with a bow.

For little creatures soft to touch,
Thank you, Father, very much!

The beetles, bugs, and butterflies,
Turtles, toads, and fireflies—

All so different, all so grand
Made by God's almighty hand!

Above my head in silence
  Fluffy clouds sail row on row:
So many shapes and sizes—
  I wonder where they go.

The ocean hides her other side,
　Her waves send forth a roar—
Leaving shells and polished stones
　Upon the sandy shore.

He formed the sun and set her high
To light the earth below.

She warms my little body
And makes the garden grow.

Tiny stars He made for me
    To glitter through the night—
For sister sun has slipped away
    And taken her great light.

Wind gently brushed by my cheek
But rarely do I hear her speak.
Through the fingers of the trees
She cools the forest with her breeze.

Throughout the branches of my oak
   Little birds peek and poke—
Their songs of praise fill the air,
   A gift from God they freely share.

And now dear loving Father
Accept the praise we bring—

And grant that we may care for
These most glorious, wondrous things.